LGBTQ Issues

Being LGBTQ

Don Nardo

ReferencePoint Press

San Diego, CA

For more information, contact:
ReferencePoint Press, Inc.
PO Box 27779
San Diego, CA 92198
www.ReferencePointPress.com

LIBRARY OF CONGRESS CATALOGING-IN-PUBLICATION DATA

Names: Nardo, Don, 1947- author.
Title: Being LGBTQ / by Don Nardo.
Description: San Diego, CA : ReferencePoint Press, [2021] | Series: LGBTQ issues | Includes bibliographical references and index.
Identifiers: LCCN 2020000091 (print) | LCCN 2020000092 (ebook) | ISBN 9781682829134 (library binding) | ISBN 9781682829141 (ebook)
Subjects: LCSH: Gays--Juvenile literature. | Sexual minorities--Juvenile literature. | Sexual orientation--Juvenile literature.
Classification: LCC HQ76.26 .N37 2020 (print) | LCC HQ76.26 (ebook) | DDC 306.76/6--dc23
LC record available at https://lccn.loc.gov/2020000091
LC ebook record available at https://lccn.loc.gov/2020000092

Contents

Introduction

Yearning for Equality

"I remember that the first time I saw all those letters jammed together," says twenty-year-old gay college student Larry in reference to the acronym *LGBTQ.* "I was fourteen and knew almost nothing about gender and sexual orientation and that sort of stuff," he goes on. "I thought: what in the world do they mean?"[1]

Larry was not the first and will likely not be the last person to be a bit confused at first sight of that now widely common acronym. The *L* stands for *lesbian* and the *G* for *gay.* The *B* means *bisexual,* often shortened to *bi,* and the *T* indicates *transgender,* frequently stated more briefly as *trans.* The *Q*, which stands for *queer,* began to appear at the end of the original acronym, *LGBT,* during the late twentieth century. According to the Lesbian, Gay, Bisexual & Transgender Community Center, an LGBTQ support group located in New York City, the term *queer* is "used by some people, particularly younger people, whose sexual orientation is not exclusively heterosexual. Typically, for those who identify as queer, the terms lesbian, gay, and bisexual are perceived to be too limiting." The *Q* can also mean *questioning.* In such a case, the center states, it "describes someone who is questioning their sexual orientation or gender identity."[2]

Speaking Out

The words people use to describe themselves get a lot of attention. But today's heightened interest in LGBTQ issues is not a result of labels. It is a result of individual people speaking out publicly about the inequality and injustice they have experienced and demanding equal treatment in all areas of their lives. About 11 million American adults, or 4.5 percent of the total population, identify as LGBTQ, according to a recent Gallup poll. Members of this community cut across all social groups: young and old, educated and noneducated, progressive and conservative, and every race, profession, and religion. As LGBTQ writer and comedian Adi Barreto puts it, "If numbers aren't your thing, I'll cut to the chase: We're everywhere."[3]

> **"If numbers aren't your thing, I'll cut to the chase: We're everywhere."[3]**
>
> —LGBTQ writer and comedian Adi Barreto

Perhaps even more important, members of this community are no longer silent—and they are no longer invisible. According to the Pew Research Center, "Nearly nine-in-ten U.S. adults (87%) say they know someone who is gay or lesbian . . . [and] 30% say they know someone who is transgender. Across most religious and demographic groups, knowing someone who is gay is quite common, with vast majorities of all groups saying they know someone who is gay."[4]

The Power of Knowledge

Despite heightened public awareness, ignorance still exists when it comes to understanding what it means to be lesbian, gay, bi, trans, or queer. Millions of people still believe old myths or labor under mistaken assumptions that do not jibe with the facts. Typical is the misguided belief that someone chooses to be gay or trans, whereas all available evidence suggests LGBTQ people are born that way.

One result of this and the many other misconceptions about being LGBTQ is that hatred, discrimination, and violence against members of the LGBTQ community continue to blight society.

About 11 million American adults identify as LGBTQ. People in this community are from all social groups: young and old, educated and non educated, and every race, profession, and religion.

Many LGBTQ people know how it feels to be treated as less than equal to heterosexual (otherwise known as "straight") people. "Crimes motivated by a bias toward gender identity," *USA Today* reported in 2019, "have generally risen since 2013, when the FBI first began reporting them."[5] Since a lack of knowledge is most often behind such crimes, it follows that knowledge—the facts about LGBTQ people and their issues—can be an antidote. According to the nonpartisan think tank the Century Foundation,

> As the American public learns more about the LGBT community, this can foster LGBT acceptance. LGBT education can be fulfilled in a variety of ways, including getting to know a family member who is gay or a friend that is transgender; it can also include consuming media that features LGBT people or characters. Seeing Caitlyn Jenner on TV, for example, can help make the change from misunderstanding to acceptance.[6]

The foundation's final point is key. When former Olympic gold medalist Bruce Jenner came out as trans in 2015 and began going by the name Caitlyn, Jenner's story did educate untold numbers of people about what being trans means. In a similar manner, other celebrities' admissions that they are not heterosexual have helped foster understanding of LGBTQ people. Only a few recent examples include singer Miley Cyrus, presidential candidate Pete Buttigieg, US Olympic track-and-field athlete Kerron Clement, *Star Trek* actor George Takei, and popular WWE wrestler Jake Atlas. As the social justice organization the Human Right Campaign puts it, "Whether it's coming out as lesbian, gay, bisexual, transgender or queer, countless actors, athletes, musicians, politicians, TV personalities and influencers have helped advance the movement for equality."[7]

> **"Seeing Caitlyn Jenner on TV . . . can help make the change from misunderstanding to acceptance."[6]**
>
> —Century Foundation

Chapter One

Coming Out

"Throughout my childhood I was a tomboy. I didn't own Barbies nor did I host tea parties," a woman in her twenties—let's call her Amy—told a University of California, Irvine, interviewer. Eventually, Amy found that she was emotionally and sexually attracted to women rather than men. In college, she recalled, "after exploring my sexuality, I found myself in a wonderful relationship with my girlfriend." But there was something lacking, she added: "As our relationship blossomed, I found myself 'hiding' my girlfriend from my family by omitting her mention. At this point, I knew that it was time to tell them. Seeing as my parents lived about four hours away, I decided I would need to take a weekend trip up north to tell them."[8]

At that important moment in her life, Amy was about to "come out," or reveal her true sexual orientation, to her family. That now common term is the shortened form of "coming out of the closet," and being "in the closet" is a reference to an LGBTQ person keeping his or her sexuality hidden. In Amy's case, she initially concealed the fact that she is a lesbian from her family.

Layers of Complexity

More specifically, because Amy is sexually attracted to someone of the same gender, she is part of the lesbian subgroup within the LGBTQ community. (While the term *gay* can be used to describe either a man or a woman, most gay women prefer to use the more traditional term *lesbian.*) Gay individuals are not the only LGBTQ people who choose to come out about their sexuality or gender identity. Some are bi, or sexually attracted to members of both genders.

A number of other LGBTQ folk are trans. Transgenderism, which is unrelated to being straight, gay, or bi, has to do with which gender one identifies with as a person. A trans person is someone who is assigned one gender at birth but at some point identifies as the other gender. Essentially, a trans man is a male trapped in a female body, and a trans woman is a female trapped in a male body.

> **"Non-binary [refers] to people who don't experience their gender(s) as completely a girl/woman or boy/man."[9]**
>
> —Trevor Project

Being LGBTQ, as well as deciding whether or not to come out, is sometimes further complicated by the fact that it is now known that human genders are not strictly binary, as once thought. Something that is binary is made up of two parts. In the realm of gender identity, throughout most of history people assumed there were only two genders—male and female. The Trevor Project, an American organization that works to reduce suicides among LGBTQ individuals, explains why that is not the case:

> Some people think that there are only two gender identities possible: boy or girl. But, in fact, thousands and thousands of people experience their gender outside of this gender binary. Some people identify as being both a boy *and* a girl, or being neither a boy nor a girl. Some folks identity as a gender that is different than boy or girl, or they don't experience gender at all. Non-binary is a term that refers to people who don't experience their gender(s) as completely a girl/woman or boy/man.[9]

Still another layer of complexity has to do with timing. LGBTQ people can come to realize their gender/orientation and decide

Transgenderism has to do with which gender one identifies with as a person. A trans person is someone who is assigned one gender but then identifies as another gender.

whether or not to come out at any age. Some do so when in their teens or twenties; for others, it does not happen until they are middle-aged; and a few are elderly when they reach that crucial point. As the Trevor Project notes, "People figure out their sexuality and gender identity at different points in their lives, and there's no wrong way to identify."[10]

The Moment of Sexual Awareness

That point when LGBTQ individuals recognize their sexual identity is often followed closely by wondering whether to come out. These individuals may initially reject the idea; moreover, that decision may remain firm for the rest of their lives. After all, some LGBTQ persons never come out. But even those who do not "go public" still come out to other LGBTQ people or certain other trusted persons in private; few people are totally closeted.

One thing is certain: the earlier in life that an LGBTQ person realizes her or his orientation—in a sense, his or her moment of sexual awareness—the longer that individual has to consider and reconsider whether to come out. That moment of awareness can happen at any point in life. Nevertheless, most LGBTQ people do recognize very early on that they are not like most of the people they know, despite not yet knowing why. As the LGBTQ center at the University of Wisconsin–Milwaukee, puts it, "Some people say they've always known that they were 'different' in some way. When they eventually realized they were [LGBTQ], many of the things they had felt growing up seemed to make sense. For others, the realization is triggered by the many changes that accompany adolescence. Some don't recognize their sexual orientation until adulthood."[11]

> **"Among gay men . . . 38% say they were younger than 10 when they first felt they were not heterosexual."[12]**
>
> —Pew Research Center

The Pew Research Center, which compiles statistics on all manners of social interactions, interviewed many thousands of LGBTQ individuals to determine the average ages at which their moments of sexual orientation awareness occurred. Its report states, "Lesbian, gay, and bisexual survey respondents were asked how old they were when they first felt they might be something other than straight or heterosexual." Pew researchers found that

> the median age across all LGBT adults is 12, although there are some differences across groups. Gay men report, on average, thinking around age 10 that they might not be straight. For both lesbians and bisexuals, the median age is 13. Among gay men, about four-in-ten (38%) say they were younger than 10 when they first felt they were not heterosexual. By comparison 23% of lesbians and 18% of bisexuals say they were younger than 10 when they first started to question their sexuality.[12]

Telling Family and Friends

Although most LGBTQ folk realize they are "different" fairly early in life, they tend not to reveal it to family and friends right away.

Pew has found that the average age of initial coming out for most LGBTQ individuals is twenty, which means that gay males who suspected they were gay at age ten waited a full decade to tell relatives and friends.

Furthermore, whether they reveal themselves as young adults or wait until later in life, a majority of those LGBTQ people who do eventually come out do not tell everyone at the same time. Most often they tell one or both parents separately from siblings and close friends. Regarding parents, Pew found that roughly 56 percent of LGBTQ adults have told their mothers about being lesbian, gay, bi, or trans. In contrast, only 39 percent of LGBTQ adults—about four in ten—reported telling their fathers about their sexual orientation or gender identity. The reasons for this difference are not totally clear, but the Pew researchers suggest that more often than not LGBTQ individuals worry that their fathers will be less understanding and accepting than their mothers about this topic.

Evidence shows that a majority of LGBTQ folks find it easier to come out to friends than to their parents. Undoubtedly this is partly because their friends are roughly the same age and therefore more easily identify with many aspects of their lives. Also, it is only natural for most people—whether LGBTQ or straight—to feel more comfortable revealing crucial secrets to friends rather than parents.

Still, occasionally LGBTQ individuals who have come out to their best friends have been surprised to receive decidedly negative reactions. One woman, now fifty-eight, recalls what happened when, at age seventeen, she came out to two close high school friends. It "was painful," she says. "They had always said they believed in everyone being their own person and living their own life, so this was a surprise when they trotted out the 'see a shrink' line and wouldn't talk to me anymore. Plus, we'd just been through the '60s and the Summer of Love and all that. I expected more open minds."[13] Another LGBTQ person—a young man—had a similar experience and recalls,

LGBTQ people tend to tell their mothers before their fathers about their sexual orientation. This could be because they believe their fathers will be less accepting of the news.

> I was sitting in my photography class with my best friend at the time and as my teacher was droning on about aperture widths and shutter speeds, I pulled my friend aside and whispered, "I need to talk to you after class about something really important. Is that cool?" . . . After class I looked him straight in the eye and told him that I was gay. That was the last time I ever talked to him. He looked at me, shook his head, and walked away. I was devastated.[14]

Why People Come Out

Considering that individuals who decide to come out sometimes get negative reactions, like the ones those two young people quoted above received, revealing one's sexual orientation can

Practical Tips on Coming Out

The Trevor Project, with branches in several large US cities, is a renowned crisis intervention group for LGBTQ people. Among other advice offered to gay, bi, and trans people, its website gives the following advice about coming out:

> It is perfectly normal to feel unsure or worried about coming out. The question of whether or not you should come out is one that only you yourself can answer. Coming out has lots of positives; it can let people in your life know about an important part of you, it can help you to feel less alone, meet new friends, as well as possibly meet people to date. There are some questions that you could ask yourself when deciding whether to come out. If you do decide to come out, who would be the first person you would come out to? . . . Is there a possibility that things may go wrong if you come out and, if there is a chance, do you have a back-up plan? If there is a chance that coming out may put you at any sort of risk or endanger your ability to continue living at home, you may want to wait to come out until you are more independent. Remember, it is your choice to come out and you do not have to come out to everybody in your life at once. You can choose who you want to come out to and when.

Trevor Support Center, "Bisexual," Trevor Project. www.thetrevorproject.org.

seem like a risky, even scary step to take. As English writer Emily Bashforth phrases it, "Regardless of what they're coming out as or who they are coming out to, this time can be riddled with fear, stress, and major anxiety. In an ideal world, no one would feel the need to come out. [Yet] coming out still happens every day."[15]

Indeed, coming out remains a persistent reality for LGBTQ people because, for a variety of reasons, a majority feel compelled to do so. For many, it is largely a matter of personal honesty. They hate the idea of living day after day with what they perceive as a lie, and they view coming out as a liberating, even empowering act. In the words of noted English actor and LGBTQ activist Ian McKellen, "I've never met a gay person who regretted coming out, including myself. Life at last begins to make sense, when you are open and honest."[16]

Another, motivation for coming out that has increasingly been cited in recent years is that it is actually healthier than constantly hiding one's true sexuality. In fact, newly released scientific data indicates that coming out is beneficial to both mental and physical health. Researchers at the Center for Studies on Human Stress at Louis H. Lafontaine Hospital in Montreal, Canada, sought to determine whether gay and bisexual people have levels of mental and physical health that are different than those of straight people. For instance, the Lafontaine researchers wondered whether gay and bi individuals who have already come out present fewer symptoms of anxiety, depression, and burnout.

After rigorous examination of the lives of nearly one hundred randomly selected gay and bi subjects, the director of the study announced its results. "Lesbians, gay men, and bisexuals who were out to family and friends," he said, "had lower levels of psychiatric symptoms . . . than those who were still in the closet."[17] That means that people who had come out were overall considerably more physically and mentally fit than people who were still in the closet. The conclusion was that because they no longer had to deal with the stress of keeping their sexuality secret, those who had come out had healthier bodies and minds overall.

> **"I've never met a gay person who regretted coming out, including myself."[16]**
>
> —Actor Ian McKellen

This fact was the central theme of a TED (technology, entertainment, and design) talk first given in 2014 by LGBTQ activist Morgana Bailey, who actually came out to the public during the lecture. She stated,

> Science has shown that LGBTQ people who consistently hide their true identities tend to live twelve fewer years than those who come out early on and admit to who they

really are. Thus, it's actually detrimental to one's life and happiness to hide one's sexual orientation. The effects of stress and social stigmas are a deadly combination. . . . I will never hide again, and I hope that by coming out I can [help] others who feel different be more themselves and more fulfilled in both their professional and personal lives.[18]

Never Too Late

Bailey says that her relationships, health, and life in general markedly improved after she came out. It is a sentiment echoed by large numbers of LGBTQ individuals who took the plunge and revealed their sexual truths. For each person who is rejected for coming out, several others report mostly positive reactions. In-

Actor Ian McKellan participates in the New York City gay pride parade in 2015. McKellan believes coming out can be a liberating experience and allows members of the LGBTQ community to live an open and honest life.

LGBTQ Siblings

Coming out can be stressful enough for an LGBTQ person, but it can be even more difficult to manage if there happen to be two LGBTQ individuals in a single family. The following recollections about such a situation are those of a young gay woman interviewed by the LGBTQ center at the University of California, Irvine.

> When my brother came out to me when I was 15, I was shocked that I didn't show him the full support I would have shown anyone else. Over time, I came to support him, and still do, but that initial failure on my part still rattled me whenever it crossed my mind. Years later . . . in college, I realized that I [am] gay. There was no way around it. I took months to deal with this revelation but later came out to my siblings, my cousins, and many of my friends. When I came out to my brother he asked me why I didn't tell him sooner and as I was giving him what I thought was my answer, I remembered when he came out to me and how I wasn't fully supportive. I realized why—another revelation. I think I have always had an inkling that I am gay and when my brother came out to me it was like he beat me to the punch. Sad to say, I was under this weird impression that there could only be one gay in the family. I was wrong.

UCI Lesbian, Gay, Bisexual, Transgender Resource Center, "Coming Out Story No. 7." University of California, Irvine, Student Affairs. https://lgbtrc.uci.edu.

deed, in many cases one or more relatives reacted better than expected. One bi man, Charlie (not his real name), considered coming out when he was eighteen and worried that his brother, in particular, would be critical. But to Charlie's pleasant surprise, the experience proved productive and liberating. "My brother has actually taken the news the best," he says, "much better than I even expected. He's met the current guy I'm dating and they hit it off well."[19]

A gay man who turned fifty-seven in 2019 recalls that his experiences with coming out have

> **"It's actually detrimental to one's life and happiness to hide one's sexual orientation."[18]**
>
> —LGBTQ activist Morgana Bailey

also been mostly positive. Back when he was twenty-one, he says, he gathered his courage and came out to his family and friends. Ever since, from time to time the subject has come up with new people he meets and he never tries to hide who he is; rather, he expects others to accept him the same way he accepts them. "Nowadays, there really is no decision," he says. "I simply have a sexual orientation the same as anyone else, and talk about my partner, etc., the same way anyone mentions their opposite-sex spouse, and there's no 'event' associated with it."[20]

A twenty-five-year-old woman who is a lesbian has the same matter-of-fact attitude. "Nearly everyone in my life knows," she explains, "and if someone new comes into my life, I tell him or her. If this person cannot accept that I am gay, then he or she does not need to be a part of my life."[21] These and other LGBTQ people like them want to live in a world in which no one discriminates about such things because people of all sexual orientations are accepted. Jim Watson, the mayor of Ottawa, Canada, feels that way and tried to set an example for others—both LGBTQ and straight—by coming out that he is gay. The words *I'm gay* took him "almost four decades to utter," he says. "But as they say, 'better late than never.' Every coming out experience is a unique journey, and it is never too late to accept yourself and live your truth."[22]

Chapter Two

Challenges for Young People

Next to parents and siblings in the home, the biggest social arena that young LGBTQ people must learn to navigate is school. They face all sorts of challenges at school, although some of those challenges are common to all young people. Others are exclusive to LGBTQ individuals. According to ULifeline, a confidential online resource center that promotes the emotional health of American school students,

> Learning to be yourself and dealing with other people's perception of you can be hard for anyone. This process can be especially stressful or tough for students who are lesbian, gay, bisexual or transgender. In fact, they can face unique issues when it comes to mental health. The discrimination LGBT students may face or the pressure they feel from their [school] or community, can put them at greater risk for emotional health struggles like depression, anxiety, substance abuse and even suicide.[23]

Facing a Traditional Social Stigma

The first challenge that LGBTQ students and other teens face is overcoming the social stigma so often associated with people who are not straight. This mean-spirited anti-LGBTQ attitude has been around for centuries. Today it is not as widespread and intense as it used to be. Yet as Sejal Singh and Laura E. Durso, experts on LGBTQ issues, point out, "LGBT people across the country continue to experience pervasive discrimination that negatively impacts all aspects of their lives. In response, LGBT people make subtle but profound changes to their everyday lives to minimize the risk of experiencing discrimination, often hiding their authentic selves." Moreover, Singh and Durso state, of the thousands of LGBTQ teens interviewed for various studies in recent years, nearly 40 percent "reported discrimination negatively impacted their school environment."[24]

Such anti-LGBTQ feelings and practices can have many injurious consequences. Some are small but are still annoying and hurtful. For instance, even the simple act of holding hands with one's girlfriend or boyfriend can become a basis for cruel treatment by insensitive classmates and bullies. One young woman describes what she and her significant other often go through in order to avoid being judged or criticized in public. "A simple expression of love and belonging is abandoned to save hassle and dodge confrontation," she says. "It makes my heart sink when I know [she] and I are going to let go of each other's hand; she gives my hand an extra little squeeze to tell me it's okay, and we let go while people pass. You make your relationship invisible."[25]

Other forms of discrimination against LGBTQ students are far worse and include verbal abuse, excluding them from normal school and social activities, and even physical violence against them. In fact, as late as 2019, the extent of such discrimination and bullying was far greater than most people realize. A survey released that year by GLSEN (formerly known as the Gay, Lesbian and Straight Education Network) stated that about 70 percent of LGBTQ students experienced verbal harassment at school because of their sexual orientation, and more than half reported harassment because of their gender expression or gender identity.

LGBTQ students must face the social stigma so often associated with people who are not straight. Sometimes this anti-LGBTQ attitude can lead to physical violence.

Moreover, nearly 30 percent of LGBTQ students were physically harassed for their sexual orientation, and almost a quarter were physically harassed for their gender expression or gender identity. More than 57 percent of LGBTQ students reported being sexually harassed.

The Negative Results of Mistreatment

The damage these sorts of actions can have on a teen's ability to learn and to his or her sense of self-worth can sometimes be severe. According to the Center for American Progress, a non-partisan public policy organization,

> This mistreatment has significant negative effects, such as causing the affected students to miss school, which leads to lower GPAs and a decreased desire to pursue post-secondary education. Worse still, according to the 2017 Youth Risk Behavior Survey, lesbian, gay, and bisexual

youth are roughly four times more likely to consider or attempt suicide than their straight peers. Similarly, transgender students are approximately four to six times more likely to attempt suicide than their cisgender [nontransgender] peers.[26]

Individual stories abound about discrimination and bullying against LGBTQ middle and high school students in recent years. In 2018 a gay teen named Daniel Segobiano had the courage to speak out and describe what he experienced at the hands of some classmates:

> I was bullied for being "too femme" and to avoid being teased I'd deepen my voice around others. In P.E. I'd always be told that I "played like a girl" or that I was not good enough to play with the other boys because I was "too gay." I was always being labeled as "too girly" for being around so many women and also shunned from masculine groups because no one wanted to be hit on by a "gay boy." To the other boys, my mannerisms were a sort of oddity that they hoped wouldn't catch on. Even my father advised me to "act more like a man" rather than more like myself.[27]

Also in 2018, high school student Ce-Lai Fong, a lesbian, recalled some of the indignities she suffered at the hands of classmates, saying,

> From a very early age, I knew that I didn't like "girly" things. I kept my hair short, I played exclusively with boys, and I didn't care that I stuck out like a sore thumb in my traditional town. However, due to my differences I was a frequent target of bullies from kindergarten all the way until high school. The bullying ranged from the more benign acts of teasing me and taking my lunch, to physical acts of aggression which consisted of shoves, pushes, and getting jumped and beaten up in the locker rooms.[28]

Fewer Dating Opportunities

Another sensitive subject for LGBTQ teens is dating. Dating can be tricky for any school-age teen, no matter what his or her sexual orientation might be. For LGBTQ teens, however, it can be especially difficult, partly because of the social stigma so often attached to being gay, bi, or trans.

> "I was a frequent target of bullies from kindergarten all the way until high school."[28]
>
> —Gay teen Ce-Lai Fong

In this regard, it usually depends on the particular school and the degree of acceptance of LGBTQ students by their teachers, administrators, and parents. In schools where there is a more tolerant atmosphere, LGBTQ dating is a less contentious issue than in schools still mired in a less tolerant atmosphere. Jade Macoy, a young woman who was a college senior in 2019, recalls that dating other females was far harder and less comfortable in high school than it became later in college. She attended a private Christian high school, she explains, where most teachers and fellow students rejected the notion

Some LGBTQ students refrain from openly dating until after they have graduated from high school or are in college. College is often a more accepting environment of LGBTQ relationships.

of same-sex dating. "It's kind of hard to openly date in an environment like that,"[29] she states. As a result of such attitudes, at least some LGBTQ high school students refrain from openly dating until after they have graduated or are in college.

Anti-LGBTQ discrimination is not the only factor that makes same-sex dating in high school awkward or even difficult. Another problem that many LGBTQ teens encounter is that most social customs surrounding school-age dating developed among and for straight people. Typically, for example, a majority of a young LGBTQ person's friends are straight and, as such, are ill equipped

Talking About LGBTQ Issues in Schools

In August 2019 Illinois became the fourth US state (after California, New Jersey, and Colorado) to require public schools to include the contributions of LGBTQ people in history classes. As reported by the *U.S. News & World Report,* Senator Heather Steans, the sponsor of Illinois's new law, remarked, "One of the best ways to overcome intolerance is through education and exposure to different people and viewpoints."

On the opposite side of the issue are a handful of states that still restrict discussion of homosexuality and LGBTQ issues in their schools. Six states (Alabama, Louisiana, Mississippi, Oklahoma, South Carolina, and Texas) "prohibit schools from teaching lesbian, gay or bisexual people or topics in a positive light in health or sexual education classes," writes *U.S. News* staff writer Casey Leins.

Some states even require that homosexuality be presented in a negative light. Liens describes an Alabama law which states that classes "must emphasize, in a factual manner and from a health perspective, that homosexuality is not a lifestyle acceptable to the general public and that homosexual conduct is a criminal offense under the laws of the state.

Casey Leins, "These States Require Schools to Teach LGBT History," *U.S. News & World Report,* August 14, 2019. www.usnews.com.

to give a gay, bi, or trans friend dating advice. One young man who came out in 2018 and wanted to find a boyfriend at school complained,

> I have no history with gay teen dating, romance, or relationships of any kind. So, of course, I want to change that, but I don't really know how to get to know a guy, how to start or continue a conversation, or anything else like that. There's one guy in particular who my friends have been trying to hook me up with, but, thanks to my lack of experience with proper communication, it all ended up a failure. I just want to know how I can change this about myself so I don't end up alone forever.[30]

Key Steps in the Dating Process

Brooklyn College health educator Ellen Friedrichs offers LGBTQ teens useful advice on how to get around such dilemmas and create healthy relationships, including romantic ones. She points out that the young man in question had already accomplished the first important step in the dating process—namely, coming out. "If you are not out," she explains, "then it is going to be a lot harder to meet guys who are gay. Plus, being out shows a certain level of confidence and confidence is really attractive to a lot of people."[31]

Similarly, Friedrichs says, an LGBTQ teen who has come out should aim for approaching other LGBTQ teens who also have come out. First, if the potential date is openly gay, she points out, "you at least know that he *could* be interested in you."[32] Also, because both parties are out, there is no need to hide the relationship, which in and of itself is liberating.

> **"Being out shows a certain level of confidence and confidence is really attractive to a lot of people."[31]**
>
> —Health educator Ellen Friedrichs

Given that an LGBTQ teen aims to find other LGBTQ teens as potential dates, where can he or she find them? According to Friedrichs and other experts, one solid approach is to get to know more fellow students in general. The more people one meets, the greater the chance that at least a few of them will be LGBTQ. So joining the school band or a club or the staff of the school paper may be a positive initial step.

One student complains that he tried joining clubs and other groups but still could not find appropriate people to date. Therefore, he turned to the internet, where dating and hookup sites are widespread. He was able to find one-time dates that way, but finding other young men who wanted a longer-term and more serious relationship remained more elusive. "I'm so sick and tired of meeting guys online who don't want a relationship," he says. "I want a boyfriend so much right now. I don't know what I have to do. The Internet seems to be the only avenue to find other gay people."[33]

Friedrichs sympathizes with the young man's frustration, as she has found that the internet has both positive and negative attributes as a place to find dates. It is "a great tool for gay teens," she writes,

> but meeting someone over the Internet will be a little different than meeting someone in person. For example, a lot of people cast a wide net when trying to meet someone online and it is possible that the guy who seems so interested in getting to know you is also sending those messages to a bunch of other people. Plus, while people don't always represent themselves honestly in real life, it is in some ways easier to claim to be someone you aren't when you don't meet in person.[34]

According to the experts, there is no magic bullet to help LGBTQ teens find fulfilling long-term relationships. Like straight students, gay, bi, and trans teens are mostly at the mercy of blind chance and being in the right place at the right time. Friedrichs sums up the reality of the situation, saying, "A lot of teens of all sexual orientations want relationships, and for some kids it just happens sooner than it does for others."[35]

Aiming for More Positive Attitudes

LGBTQ teens are very much like straight teens in another way. Namely, they desire to have as normal, positive, and productive a time as possible when they attend middle school and high school. The fact that so many LGBTQ teens find themselves dealing with discrimination, dating difficulties, loneliness, depression, and other negative outcomes demonstrates that there is much room for improvement in their school lives.

Evidence from various studies of the situation indicate that to encourage and achieve more positive attitudes by and about LGBTQ teens, members of three separate groups must work together. The first group consists of LGBTQ teens themselves. According to ULifeline, school-age gay, bi, and trans people should

LGBTQ students should try to surround themselves with supportive people. These might include sympathetic teachers and school administrators.

> **"Remember that others' reactions to your sexual identity or orientation are not your fault."[36]**
>
> —ULifeline, an online site that promotes good health for teens

first try to surround themselves with supportive people. These might include other LGBTQ students or sympathetic parents, teachers, and administrators. Such supporters understand the problems that LGBTQ teens face and can offer helpful advice to make going to school safer and more rewarding.

Also, young LGBTQ persons should not fall into the trap of believing that they are somehow sick or inferior, which are baseless claims typically made by ill-informed individuals and groups. "Remember," ULifeline advises LGBTQ teens, such misinformation "has nothing to do with you. Society creates and perpetuates stigmas about many groups. Remember that others' reactions to your sexual identity or orientation are not your fault, and say nothing about the person you are"[36]

The second group that can help LGBTQ teens adjust better to school life consists of their fellow classmates and other friends. A straight teen can support a gay, bi, or trans friend or acquaintance first by being a good listener and sympathizing with their problems. When talking to an LGBTQ person, ULifeline says,

> don't interrupt and remain open to what they're saying. Avoid judging them, and try to put yourself in their shoes. Get educated. Learn more about concerns that LGBT individuals might have. This helps you better understand what your friend is going through and know how to help him or her. Challenge the stigma. Try not to make derogatory comments about LGBT individuals. Even jokes just further stereotypes and stigma. And speak up when others make comments or jokes.[37]

The third group of supporters of LGBTQ teens is composed of teachers, parents, and other adults with whom teens normally interact. In 2018 gay youth Parker Reyes, who had recently gradu-

Safety Tips for Online Dating

Some LGBTQ teens have bad experiences with dating in school, so they turn to online dating sites. Some are legitimate and well vetted, but others are anonymous, unregulated, and shady. Those in the latter category can end up causing teens—both LGBTQ and straight—more trouble than they bargained for. LiveAbout, a site that offers young people sound advice on social matters, offers the following safety tips:

> It is extremely easy to lie about who you are in an online profile. You can post any picture you want and claim it is of you. Predators do this without remorse. They pose as teenaged girls when they are really grown men and pictures posted alongside the false profile fool other users (this is called "catfishing"). . . . Wanna play it safe in the online dating world? Here are the Dos and Don'ts of Online Relationships for Teens: Don't give out your real name, address, birthdate, and location to anyone whom you met over the Internet. That person may not be who they are portraying to be, so they don't need to know personal details about you. Don't meet up with online "friends" alone. If you choose to meet someone online in person, be sure to take a friend with you and to meet in a very public place, like a shopping mall or a crowded Starbucks. Don't send anyone money who you have met online. There are a ton of scam artists out there who know enticing tricks to take advantage of teenagers.

Mike Hardcastle, "Meeting People Online—Online Safety Tips for Teens," LiveAbout, July 14, 2017. www.liveabout.com.

ated from high school, concisely summarized the role that adults should ideally play in the lives of LGBTQ teens:

> Educators and parents need to remember that LGBTQ youth still to this day grow up surrounded by cultural images and cues that suggest to them that their identity is evil or inherently wrong. The number one thing I believe parents and educators can do to combat [discrimination

against] LGBTQ individuals is to talk about LGBTQ issues and people in a very humanizing way. Parents and educators are points of authority for youth and so it is their job to set the tone, expectations, and acceptable behavior pertaining to the humane and ethical treatment of these students' queer peers. Setting the tone and combating the negative social narratives about LGBTQ people is how educators and parents can create more inclusive and equitable spaces for LGBTQ youth.[38]

Interviewed in 2018 for GLAAD (formerly the Gay & Lesbian Alliance Against Defamation), another recent high school graduate, Ose Arheghan, urged parents and teachers to educate themselves about LGBTQ issues. "Much of the negativity I experienced when I was younger," he said, "could've been avoided with education and tolerance."[39]

Chapter Three

Creating a Family

Today when people mention LGBTQ issues relating to parenting and families, they may be referring to one of two scenarios. One involves gay, bi, or trans children who grow up in homes in which the parents and all or most of the siblings are straight. The other scenario, which used to be rare but is fast expanding in the United States and other Western nations, is one in which LGBTQ couples marry and have families of their own.

More Alike than Different

Each of these family scenarios has certain unique circumstances and issues that the other lacks. But to many people's surprise, the ways they are alike far outnumber the ways they differ. For example, all available surveys indicate that the vast majority of marriages—whether heterosexual or same sex—are based on strong feelings of love between the spouses.

Second, many gay and lesbian individuals express a desire to have children. In 2019 the Family Equality Council, an organization that promotes fair and equal treatment for LGBTQ parents and families, announced the findings of its landmark LGBTQ Family Building Survey. The study found that 48 percent of LGBTQ millennials are actively planning to have children and create families. That proportion, which is steadily growing each year, is already statistically comparable

> **"Relationships of lesbian and gay couples are just as supportive [of children] as those [of] heterosexual parents."[40]**
>
> —University of Virginia scholar Charlotte J. Patterson

to the 55 percent of non-LGBTQ millennials who are engaged in family building.

Still another way that families headed by LGBTQ parents are virtually the same as families created by straight people is that both kinds of parents love their kids and want what is best for them. Study after study has shown that LGBTQ parents tend to establish stable, loving homes no less often than straight parents do. This flies in the face of the negative stereotypes and myths that for decades claimed that families established by gay couples were certain to be unstable and unsafe for children. According to the widely respected University of Virginia social scientist Charlotte J. Patterson, "The evidence suggests that relationships of lesbian and gay couples are just as supportive and that home environments provided by lesbian and gay parents are just as likely as those provided by heterosexual parents to enable psychosocial growth among family members."[40]

The Society for the Psychological Study of Social Issues, an international group of some three thousand psychologists and scientists, agrees. There is no scientific basis, its spokespeople say, to suggest that LGBTQ adults on the whole are not equally fit to marry or to become parents of healthy and happy offspring. Furthermore, they say,

> there is no empirical foundation [factual basis] for concluding that lesbian mothers or gay fathers should not become parents on the basis of their sexual orientation. Being involved in a gay and lesbian relationship is unrelated to a person's ability to care for children. Scientific surveys show that lesbian and heterosexual women share similar approaches to child rearing. Numerous studies indicate that gay fathers are no different from heterosexual fathers in their ability to parent and to foster the healthy development of their children.[41]

Children of Gay Parents Tell Their Stories

> "Growing up with lesbian moms has been the most normal thing to ever happen to me."[42]
>
> —College student Katie Hershey van Horn

Bolstering the wealth of scientific evidence are thousands of testimonials from the teenage or grown children of LGBTQ parents. "Growing up with lesbian moms has been the most normal thing to ever happen to me, honestly," says Katie Hershey van Horn, who was twenty-one and attending the University of Hawaii in 2019. "It's so brutally normal! I have to do chores around the house, walk our dog, feed our cats and do my own laundry. I was raised like any other kid: always say 'please' and 'thank you,' don't put your elbows on the table, and don't litter!"[42]

Firefighter Michael Arden-Sonego, who was twenty-four in 2019, grew up in a situation similar to that of Katie. The main difference was that he has two dads instead of two moms. Again, what stands out in his recollections is the relative normalcy of

Studies have shown that LGBTQ parents tend to establish stable, loving homes just as often as straight parents do. This goes against negative claims to the contrary.

The Two-Dads Dynamic

Government statistics show that each year the number of male same-sex couples that start families increases. Andrew Leland, a professor at Southern Illinois University, has extensively studied the unique approach taken by two gay men in raising children. He reports that "two-dad households can challenge the 1940s Norman Rockwell image of gendered parenting, just like heterosexual couples can." Moreover, he explains,

> some of these men even take on responsibilities based on skills and strength, rather than who fits the socially and culturally constructed mold of being more "motherly" or "fatherly." And that's where the parenting of gay dads may differ from a traditional heterosexual household, as my research and the work of other scholars suggests. While interviewing and spending time with 22 gay-fathered families living in the Northeast, I have learned that they're apt to step up. [They frequently] become involved as classroom parents, voluntarily assisting teachers, reading books or leading singalongs. Some take leadership roles by becoming active PTA members or organizing events that go beyond their children's classes. In some cases, gay fathers become PTA presidents or serve on school boards. . . . Gay dads prefer schools and communities that are safe and inclusive. As my research suggests, living in an inclusive community makes them more likely to engage. Beyond that, they want lawmakers bent on barring them from fatherhood to see that two-dad families are for the most part just like any other family.

Andrew Leland, "How Families with 2 Dads Raise Their Kids," The Conversation, June 11, 2019. http://theconversation.com.

his home life, which included all the usual expected features and benefits of having a large extended family. He recalls,

> When the social worker told me that the couple that wanted to adopt my brothers and me was two men, she waited for some reaction, but I didn't care. I just wanted to live

somewhere I could call home, somewhere where I could finally relax and know my brothers and I were going to be taken care of. Besides new parents, we got a big family with cousins, grandparents, aunts, uncles and four dogs. My parents are good-hearted people who have worked hard to give us many opportunities and I am very grateful to have them as parents.[43]

Nineteen-year-old Massachusetts resident George, another young man who was raised by two male parents, also stresses how normal it seemed. In addition, he shatters the once widely believed myth that two gay parents will likely induce their children to be gay too. "My dads always encouraged me to be myself," he states.

> At one point we had "the talk"—you know, about sex stuff—and they said they didn't care whether I turned out to be straight or gay, as long as I was kind, and honest, and happy. They never once suggested that being gay was preferable to being straight, and even if they *had,* it wouldn't have made any difference since I'm straight. Even back in grade school I knew I liked girls, so there was never any question about it in my mind.[44]

George's positive personal experience with being raised by two fathers has been mirrored in the findings of numerous scientific studies. In 2019 Cornell University researchers announced the results of an extensive survey they had conducted. "We identified 79 scholarly studies that met our criteria for adding to knowledge about the well-being of children with gay or lesbian parents," a university spokesperson stated. Of those studies, almost all "concluded that children of gay or lesbian parents fare no worse than other children. Taken together, this research forms an overwhelming scholarly consensus, based on over three decades of peer-reviewed research, that having a gay or lesbian parent does not harm children."[45]

An Impressive Number of Children

First-person accounts like those of Katie, Michael, and George have proved crucial in recent years. Such stories have been instrumental in changing national perceptions of both same-sex marriages and child rearing by LGBTQ parents. Indeed, testimony given to the US Congress by the children of LGBTQ couples helped to convince Supreme Court Justice Anthony Kennedy to support LGBTQ equality and justice. He became the swing vote in the court's milestone June 2015 ruling that made gay marriage legal in all fifty states.

> **"Having a gay or lesbian parent does not harm children."[45]**
>
> — 2019 Cornell University study

Following that long-awaited achievement of marriage equality, large numbers of LGBTQ couples married. Moreover, the legitimacy and stability that being married afforded those couples made the prospect of raising children—which before had been a hard hill to climb—suddenly seem within reach. Various experts predicted that the high court's ruling would likely lead to a major upsurge in adoption and child rearing among LGBTQ-headed families, and that growth spurt occurred as expected. What is more, it happened in a big way. According to data collected by the Family Equality Council and other groups that monitor such trends, between 2015 and 2019 there was a whopping 44 percent increase in the number of young LGBTQ couples either starting or seriously considering starting families.

Actual raw numbers of parents and children involved in this trend are somewhat unclear. But the Family Equality Council estimates that close to 4 million LGBTQ millennials began raising children between 2015 and 2019. Older gay, bi, and trans couples also started families during that period, although in smaller numbers. (Some of the older couples already had one or more children before the advent of marriage equality.) Together, both younger and older LGBTQ parents began raising an impressive number of children. According to the American Civil Liberties Union, which collects statistics about the members of minority groups in the United States, in 2019 the total number of children nationwide living with at least one gay parent was no less than 6 million and may have been as high as 14 million.

Adoption

These figures are not surprising. Like straight parents, gay and bi parents possess the same common human desire to have, love, and nurture their own children. The sheer number of marriages and volume of child rearing among LGBTQ couples that have occurred since marriage equality clearly bears this out. Furthermore, experts expect the proportion of LGBTQ parents having children to continue growing in the near future until it closely matches the percentage of straight parents doing so.

Although there are many similarities between straight and LGBTQ families, some significant differences exist between them as well. One of the more marked of those differences is the manner in which gay and bi couples, especially younger ones, actually have children. Before the 2015 Supreme Court ruling on marriage equality, most of the gay and bi people who had children were not "out" socially. The few that were out tended to adopt. But most of those still in the closet had children through marriage to someone of the opposite sex. That person may or may not have known that her or his spouse was gay or bi. The Family Equality Council's LGBTQ Family Building Survey found that 73 percent of these older LGBTQ folks rearing children had them via sexual intercourse.

In contrast, far fewer present-day millennials and other young gay and bi people with children are choosing to have those offspring through intercourse. The continuingly growing majority have been turning to alternate methods. One is the old societal standby of adoption. Some have opted to adopt through the child welfare system, meaning they have become foster

Supreme Court justice Anthony Kennedy (pictured) became the swing vote in the court's milestone 2015 ruling that made gay marriage legal in all fifty states.

parents. A minority of these couples have opted to foster one or more children on a long-term basis; the majority, however, eventually applied to formally adopt those kids, which is a process called public adoption. In public adoptions, the state pays most of the expenses. In contrast, a larger proportion of LGBTQ couples seeking to adopt choose private adoption, in which they go through a private adoption agency. In private adoptions, the couple pays for most of the expenses, including the fee for the attorney who negotiates with the agency and birth mother.

Statistics show that adoption is far more popular with same-sex couples than it is with straight couples. In fact, same-sex couples are at least four times more likely to adopt than heterosexual couples, the public policy group the Williams Institute states. The US Census Bureau and other government agencies estimate that in 2019 approximately sixty-six thousand adopted children in the United States were living with male or female gay parents. Moreover, that number represented 4 percent of all the country's adopted children. Of the fifty states, California led the way, with about sixteen thousand of the LGBTQ adoptions.

Reproductive Technology

Another route taken by a growing number of lesbian parents is to employ reproductive technologies. One such technology is intrauterine insemination. It involves implanting sperm (from a sperm bank or known donor) directly into the ovulating potential mother's uterus. It is hoped that then the natural occurring process will take over and the sperm will make its way to the fallopian tubes and there fertilize an egg.

In another approach—in vitro fertilization (IVF)—doctors remove an egg from a woman's body and fertilize it in a lab using donated sperm. They then implant the fertilized egg into the woman's uterus. Still another approach is a variation known as reciprocal in vitro fertilization; it consists of taking an egg for IVF from one partner of a lesbian couple and implanting the fertilized egg in the other partner. Many lesbian couples opt for this approach because they feel that having both mothers directly involved in the process creates an extra emotional bond, even though the child will only be genetically related to the egg donor partner.

An approach used by a growing number of male gay couples is to have one of the would-be fathers donate sperm. Then, using either intrauterine insemination or IVF, the sperm or fertilized egg is implanted in a surrogate, or stand-in woman. She is either a volunteer (usually a friend or relative of the men) or is a professional surrogate who is paid for her services. She carries the baby to term and delivers it to the two fathers.

In addition, both male and female gay couples may opt for creating a child through traditional intercourse. In this approach,

Statistics show that adoption is far more popular with same-sex couples than it is with straight couples. Same-sex couples are over four times more likely to adopt than straight couples.

one of the would-be fathers or mothers has sex with a volunteer of the opposite gender strictly to achieve pregnancy. The LGBTQ Family Building Survey found that fewer LGBTQ couples choose this route. Instead, between 2015 and 2019, 63 percent of them opted for either adoption or the use of reproductive technologies.

Everyone Deserves a Chance

By whatever means that same-sex couples end up having children, studies indicate that most such LGBTQ families tend to be stable and nurturing. Indeed, research shows that children raised by same-sex parents achieve success both in school and after graduating at rates virtually identical to those of children raised by heterosexual couples. Furthermore, the studies show, the sexual orientation of the parents has no bearing on the sexual orientation of the children. As the website GayAdoption.org puts it, "Children are more influenced by their parents' relationship with each other than with the sexual orientation of their parents." Also, "Good parenting is influenced by the parent's ability to create a loving and nurturing home."[46]

The Problem of LGBTQ Homelessness

The Homelessness Policy Research Institute (HPRI), based in Los Angeles, is a group of thirty scholars and policy makers who research homelessness in Los Angeles County and suggest policies to remedy that problem. The HPRI and other similar research organizations have found that one of the largest single causes of homelessness among young people—in both Los Angeles and in the United States as a whole—is due to straight parents throwing their LGBTQ children out of the house to fend for themselves. These groups estimate that an incredible 20 to 40 percent of homeless teens and young adults in the country identify as LGBTQ. Forced onto the streets by their own parents, most of these young people are traumatized, and many of them get involved in crime or suffer violent attacks. In a 2019 report, the HPRI stated,

> Although exact numbers are hard to find due to uneven disclosure of sexual orientation and gender identity from youth, somewhere between 20 to 40% (300,000 to 600,000) of youth experiencing homelessness identify as LGBTQ compared to 4 to 10% of the total youth population. Estimates suggest that LGBTQ youth are anywhere from 2 to 13 times more likely to experience homelessness compared to heterosexual and cisgender youth. Studies also find that leaving home due to conflict with guardians over sexual orientation or gender expression is the primary reason for housing instability among LGBTQ youth. Once they leave home, LGBTQ youth experience higher rates of violence, physical and mental health degradation, and exploitation when compared to other youth experiencing homelessness.

Homelessness Policy Research Institute, "LGBTQ Youth Experiencing Homelessness," Price Center for Social Innovation, University of Southern California, August 19, 2019. https://socialinnovation.usc.edu.

> **"Good parenting is influenced by the parent's ability to create a loving and nurturing home."[46]**
>
> —GayAdoption.org

Once more, that reality is better expressed by the children themselves than by studies and stats. A moving example made the national news in 2015, when the Supreme Court was still debating whether to legalize gay marriage. Twelve-year-old Californian Daniel Martinez-Leffew, who, along with his sister, had been adopted and raised by two dads, found out that a member of the high court had two adopted children. Daniel wrote a letter to that justice in hopes of garnering support for marriage equality. "I was lucky to be adopted by two guys I can both call 'Dad,'" the young man wrote. "They give me and my sister so much love. . . . It's important that all families are protected and valued. In our country, we may not all be the same but we are all Americans who deserve an equal chance at bettering our lives."[47]

Chapter Four

At Work and in the Public Sphere

In addition to the difficulties that many LGBTQ people have historically experienced in their home lives and at school, they often encounter other problems at work and in public settings. Since the start of the twenty-first century the LGBTQ community has made impressive strides toward equality and fair treatment. Yet the sober reality is that its members continue to face various forms of discrimination in the workplace and public sphere.

Ongoing workplace discrimination against LGBTQ individuals was revealed in a major 2017 national survey by the Center for American Progress (CAP). Among those interviewed—representing a broad range of races, ethnicities, income brackets, and sexual orientations—almost 20 percent of gay and bi workers reported losing a promotion based on their sexual orientation. Gender identity also frequently comes into play in this regard. In the same survey, close to 30 percent of trans workers said they were recently fired, not hired, or denied a promotion because they are trans.

Multiple surveys show that in public life outside the workplace, LGBTQ discrimination can be less obvious on the surface but no less insidious and hurtful. Of the LGBTQ people interviewed in those studies, many said that prejudice and unfair treatment has at one time or another negatively affected their health, economic security, or overall sense of psychological well-being. They cited discrimination in housing, in the use of public transportation and bathroom facilities, and in access to health care services of various kinds. Evidence suggests this sort of discrimination is steadily decreasing in the United States, even if not as swiftly as LGBTQ Americans would like.

Adverse Workplace Experiences

In fact, for many adult LGBTQ Americans, the principal arena in which they experience discrimination remains the workplace. According to a comprehensive 2017 study by the prestigious Robert Wood Johnson Foundation and the Harvard T.H. Chan School of Public Health, fully one-fifth of LGBTQ American workers have experienced unfair treatment when applying for a job. Also, some 22 percent of these workers report being paid less than straight workers for doing the same work.

> "When you're perceived as feminine . . . you get excluded from relationships that improve your career."[48]
>
> —David, a gay man who works for a large company

These sorts of overt discrimination are only part of the story, however. Even when LGBTQ workers are not turned down for or fired from a job, some say that anti-LGBTQ biases shape their lives in diverse ways. "I couldn't be fired for being gay," says David, a gay man who works at a Fortune 500 company that has a written nondiscrimination policy. However, he explains,

> when partners at the firm invite straight men to [play] squash or [for] drinks, they don't invite the women or gay men. I'm being passed over for opportunities that could lead to being promoted. I'm trying to minimize the bias against me by changing my presentation in the corporate world. I lower my voice in meetings to make it sound less feminine and avoid wearing anything but a black suit. . . . When you're perceived as feminine—whether you're a woman or a gay man—you get excluded from relationships that improve your career.[48]

Studies show that nearly 30 percent of trans workers said they were recently fired, not hired, or denied a promotion because they are trans.

David's experiences are partially based on the fact that he is out. Many LGBTQ American workers remain in the closet for fear of prejudice. A 2019 Human Rights Campaign survey found that 46 percent of LGBTQ workers in the United States are closeted in the workplace. A North Carolina woman named Maria, who identifies as queer, is among them. In an interview with CAP, she says that she likes her job a lot but worries about what might happen if she reveals she is not straight. "I wonder whether I would be let go if the higher-ups knew about my sexuality,"[49] she remarks.

The decision not to come out at work is often part of a pattern of choices that are intended to make life easier but often, ultimately, do not achieve that goal. Some of these workers describe

Denying LGBTQ People Service

Should businesses be required to treat LGBTQ customers like all other customers? This issue came up in Colorado in 2012 when a baker cited his religious beliefs for not agreeing to bake a custom cake for a gay couple's wedding reception. The baker stated that his religion teaches that marriage should only take place between a man and a woman. The couple sued the baker, contending he had violated state laws prohibiting discrimination based on sexual orientation. State courts agreed with the gay couple but the baker appealed these decisions.

The case eventually went before the US Supreme Court. In June 2018 the Supreme Court decided in favor of the baker, citing anti-religious bias by the state agency that originally considered the case. The justices did not address the issue of whether religious liberty claims entitle other businesses to refuse service to LGBTQ people. Speaking for the majority, Justice Anthony Kennedy wrote, "The laws and the Constitution can, and in some instances must, protect gay persons and gay couples in the exercise of their civil rights. But religious and philosophical objections to gay marriage are protected views and in some instances protected forms of expression."

Quoted in David Smith and Lucia Graves, "Supreme Court Sides with Baker Who Refused to Make Gay Wedding Cake," *Guardian*, 2018. www.theguardian.com.

how the atmosphere in their hometowns is unfriendly toward the LGBTQ community. This, they say, prompted them to look for jobs in cities miles away that are known for being more LGBTQ friendly. Thus, an unknown proportion of LGBTQ Americans feel that they must regularly spend extra time and money to commute to work in order to avoid discrimination.

Concern about discrimination can also adversely affect the manner in which LGBTQ people plan for the future or better their professional positions and opportunities. A gay California college student named Rafael told CAP that he had opted "to apply to law schools only in LGBT-safe cities or states." He said he realized that this meant the quality of his education would be less than it would be if he attended the schools he preferred. But he felt he had no other choice. In his words, "I did not think I would be safe being an openly gay man, especially a gay man of color, in some places."[50] According to the organization Catalyst, which advocates for women in the workplace, in these and other ways, LGBTQ Americans "often cover or downplay aspects of their authentic selves . . . in order to avoid discrimination."[51]

A Public Uproar

In addition to unfair treatment in the workplace, discrimination against LGBTQ people has long been common in places of public accommodation, including restaurants, hotels, government offices, and public bathrooms. Members of the gay community felt the sting of such prejudice regularly until education and more enlightened public attitudes during the late twentieth century and early 2000s made it a good deal less prevalent. However, even as that progress was happening, issues surrounding transgender people began to make the news. Before the 2000s, most Americans had been unaware of even the existence of trans people. Moreover, the concept of a person's gender identity being different than his or her genitals at birth can initially seem counterintuitive and difficult to grasp.

As a result, it was easy for misinformation, fear, and prejudice relating to trans individuals to spread. Many Americans, including legislators in a number of states, worried that allowing trans people to use their preferred gender's public restrooms would lead to sexual assaults against women by men dressed as women. Particularly worrisome to many parents was the notion of trans students using their gender-preferred school restroom.

This controversy entered the public sphere in a big way in 2015 and 2016, when the legislatures of eight states, including North Carolina, Mississippi, and Texas proposed so-called bathroom bills. (Some US cities also considered them.) These statutes were intended to prohibit trans people from using public restrooms labeled with their gender identities. That means that a male-to-female trans person could not use a "ladies' room," and a female-to-male trans person was not allowed inside a "men's room."

Not surprisingly, trans people felt they were the targets of blatant discrimination. Since public restrooms exist in schools, restaurants, hotels, department stores, and even town squares, they felt they were being kept from using public accommodations open to nontransgender individuals. A public uproar occurred, with loud support for both sides of the issue.

From Negative to Positive

The sometimes angry debates over the restroom issue had a perhaps unexpected yet welcome outcome for trans people: for the first time ever, large numbers of Americans learned about what it means to be trans. As Jay Michaelson, a legal affairs columnist at the Daily Beast website, puts it, "Being transgender is not a whim. You can't just put on a wig and say you consider yourself female—as one right-wing protester at [a] Target [store] did recently." To be transgender "is an identity," he adds. "These are facts; not opinions."[52] As more and more people were exposed to those facts, they came to see the bathroom bills as hysterical overreactions. Indeed, of all the state restroom laws proposed, only one—in North Carolina—passed in March 2016. The others rapidly lost steam and died in the legislatures.

Moreover, the North Carolina law immediately proved to be hugely unpopular. In addition to protests by trans and other LGBTQ people, all the major civil rights groups condemned it. At the same time, a wide range of corporations, entertainers, and sports teams expressed their disdain for the law, which they claimed clearly discriminated against trans people. Many of these groups and individuals threatened to take their business to other states. That, they pointed out, would cause North Carolina to lose tens of millions of dollars in needed revenue. The state's legislators eventually reversed course. In March 2017, a year after the law had passed, they repealed it.

> **"Being transgender is not a whim. . . . [It] is an identity. These are facts; not opinions."[52]**
>
> —Daily Beast columnist Jay Michaelson

Another unexpected outcome of the bathroom bill controversy was that it actually ended

In 2015 and 2016 eight states proposed so-called bathroom bills that prohibited male-to-female trans people from using a "women's room," and female-to-male trans people from using a "men's room."

up strengthening antidiscrimination laws and, in the process, expanding legal protections for trans and other LGBTQ people. In 2018 three states—Hawaii, New Jersey, and Vermont—passed pro-trans laws. The Vermont version ordered that all public restrooms in the state be labeled *gender neutral*, which nullified any further controversy. It also afforded trans people the dignity of being treated like everyone else. That same year, Massachusetts voters overwhelmingly affirmed that all forms of gender discrimination in public facilities should be banned.

This trend continued in 2019. That year, only a single state—Indiana—proposed a law similar to the bathroom bills, but it did not pass. Further rejecting that approach, the year also witnessed legislatures in seven other states working to expand the rights of trans and other LGBTQ individuals.

Equality for LGBTQ People at Last?

On May 17, 2019, a bill known as the Equality Act passed by a wide majority in the US House of Representatives. At the close of that year it had not yet come up for a vote in the Senate, which must pass the bill for it to then be signed by the president into law. The nonpartisan, widely respected Human Rights Campaign provides this informative overview of the bill:

> The Equality Act would provide consistent and explicit non-discrimination protections for LGBTQ people across key areas of life, including employment, housing, credit, education, public spaces and services, federally funded programs, and jury service. The Equality Act would amend existing civil rights law—including the Civil Rights Act of 1964, the Fair Housing Act, the Equal Credit Opportunity Act, the Jury Selection and Services Act, and several laws regarding employment with the federal government—to explicitly include sexual orientation and gender identity as protected characteristics. The legislation also amends the Civil Rights Act of 1964 to prohibit discrimination in public spaces and services and federally funded programs on the basis of sex. . . . These important updates would strengthen existing protections for everyone. Decades of civil rights history show that civil rights laws are effective in decreasing discrimination because they provide strong federal remedies targeted to specific vulnerable groups. By explicitly including sexual orientation and gender identity in these fundamental laws, LGBTQ people will finally be afforded the exact same protections as other covered characteristics under federal law.

Human Rights Campaign, "The Equality Act," October 1, 2019. www.hrc.org.

Unequal Treatment in Health Care

Numerous facts and statistics collected between 2017 and 2019, including CAP's major survey, show that health care is another area in which LGBTQ rights lag. The data indicates that some doctors and other health care workers, as well as health insurance companies, discriminate against them on a regular basis. According to the evidence, transgender individuals are particularly vulnerable to unequal treatment in health care. Moreover, when turned away, they often have a hard time finding alternative medical services.

The CAP study tried to clarify the specific ways that some members of the medical community discriminate against LGBTQ people. The survey asked respondents to describe their personal experiences with health care–related discrimination in the previous year. Among LGBTQ people in general, 8 percent said that a doctor or other health care provider refused to see them; 7 percent responded that a provider also refused to treat the LGBTQ person's partner or child; and 9 percent said that a doctor or other health care provider did treat them but repeatedly verbally accosted them during treatment.

These abuses by health care providers were even more pronounced in the specific cases in which the patients were transgender. A disturbing 29 percent, or almost a third, of the respondents recounted how a doctor or other health care provider refused to see them simply because they were trans. One female-to-male trans person, who now calls himself Arthur, explained that he had moved to a new town and had not yet chosen a local doctor. When he suddenly came down with flu-like symptoms, he phoned a doctor's office to make an appointment and had a rude awakening. "I made the mistake of letting them know that I'm trans," he recalls.

"I made the mistake of letting them know that I'm trans."[53]

—Arthur, a female-to-male trans person

> Right after that they told me I would have to see a different doctor, and when I asked why, they said he doesn't treat transgender people, to which I asked why again, and at that point they claimed they had to go and hung up on me. Now I realize it was just as well I didn't end up seeing him. It's pretty clear he's not a very good person, so how can he be a good doctor?[53]

LGBTQ people often experience discrimination when seeking medical care. Medical schools are introducing programs that help medical students better prepare to treat LGBTQ patients.

Toward a More Hopeful Future

Arthur's unwelcome experience illustrates only the most blatant way that some health care providers discriminate against trans people. CAP study respondents described other negative—and hurtful—encounters with doctors. For instance, 23 percent of the providers refused to call a patient by the name he or she had adopted during transitioning. Moreover, 21 percent of those doctors or other providers used harsh or abusive language when speaking to trans patients.

No less disturbing were cases in which trans patients were seeking treatment directly related to their transitioning, including getting hormone injections. According to the CAP survey, 12 percent of the doctors or other health care professionals declined to provide the patients with any sort of care related to gender transitioning. Dylan, a trans resident of Oregon, remembers going to see a physician in his hometown to receive hormone treatments as part of his ongoing female-to-male transition. The doctor claimed to be "uncomfortable" prescribing hormones to trans patients. His solution, Dylan says, "was to send trans people 90 miles (one way) to the university hospital to get hormones." The treatment at that hospital, Dylan explains,

> was horrendous, and I was in that situation only because the doctor in my midwestern hometown feared a waiting room with a 6 foot 4 person in a dress with a beard, hairy legs, and a protruding Adam's apple making others uncomfortable. That fear led to discrimination against a class of people already too often burdened with low income, unmet health needs, and mental health issues.[54]

These negative experiences can and do lead to harmful outcomes in some cases. Some LGBTQ people who encounter repeated discrimination in health care, the workplace, and other areas of the public sphere experience various mental health issues. These can include depression, post-traumatic stress disorder, and, in the most extreme cases, suicide.

> **"Like everyone, [transgender people] deserve equality, fairness, and dignity when seeking medical care."[55]**
>
> —The magazine *The Humanist*

On the positive side, a number of medical schools have recognized these problems and have addressed them by introducing programs that help medical students better prepare to treat trans and other LGBTQ patients. According to the magazine the *Humanist,*

> The University of Louisville, in Kentucky, created a medical program in 2015 called the Equality Project, which trains students in common healthcare treatments for transgender [people]. Students learn about transgender terminology and LGBTQ patient care at Case Western Reserve in Ohio, and New York's Mount Sinai Hospital offers fellowships in transgender care. . . . These programs signal a hopeful future toward better and more accessible healthcare options for transgender patients, who, like everyone, deserve equality, fairness, and dignity when seeking medical care and treatment.[55]

Chapter Five

Faced with Violence

In the early evening of January 19, 2019, two young gay men, Tristan Perry and Spencer Deehring, exited a bar in Austin, Texas, where they had enjoyed a couple of drinks and watched some football on the bar's television. They held hands as they strolled down the street. Suddenly a stranger approached them and screamed a homophobic slur. Taken off guard, Perry and Deehring were unprepared for what happened next. The stranger signaled to three other men, and the four launched a brutal attack on the gay couple. The attackers threw their victims to the ground and kicked them both in the head. The perpetrators were later arrested and punished, but Perry and Deehring were injured so badly that they had to be hospitalized.

Later that year, on June 10, twenty-three-year-old Chanel Scurlock, a transgender woman in North Carolina, set out to meet with someone she had corresponded with on Facebook. She never reached her destination. The next day police found her bullet-ridden body in a field. Her homicide marked the ninth known murder of a black trans woman in the United States in 2019.

These two crimes made up only a fragment of an epidemic of anti-LGBTQ violence that gripped the United States between 2016 and 2019. According to the Federal Bureau of Investigation (FBI), hate crimes in general—including those motivated by racial, religious, and sexuality differences—reached a twenty-seven-year high in 2018 and 2019. Of these, the FBI's statistics show that 17 percent were committed because the victims were gay or bi. Another 2.4 percent were motivated by gender-identity bias, or the fact that the victims were trans. (Although 2.4 percent may seem small at first glance, it is actually alarmingly high considering that trans people make up less than half of 1 percent of the country's population.)

The ongoing rise in anti-LGBTQ violence is reflected in the raw numbers of hate crimes and other violent acts. In 2017, for instance, the FBI reported 118 violent crimes against trans people. That number increased to 184 in 2018 and has since continued to climb. Part of the problem, contends Xavier Persad, a senior legislative counsel for the Human Rights Campaign, is the lack of sufficient laws with which to charge the perpetrators. As late as October 2019, he points out, only twenty states and Washington, DC, had laws that address hate crimes based on sexual orientation and gender identity. The rising crime rate, he adds, "reminds us of the importance of the work left to be done to protect LGBTQ people."[56]

Violent Bullying in Schools

The torrent of anti-LGBTQ violence often begins in schools, with the more severe incidents of bullying endured by gay, bi, and trans students. Although name-calling, threats to harm someone, and excluding someone from various school activities are all forms of bullying, they do not rise to the level of physical violence. Although violent bullying happens less often than these other types of bullying, it is far from rare. The United Nations Educational, Scientific and Cultural Organization estimates that 32 percent of students in US and other North American schools suffer at least one physical attack each year. Of these victims, a high proportion are LGBTQ people. In a similar vein, studies conducted by GLSEN indicate that more than 20 percent of trans students are bullied

> **"I've been shoved into lockers."**[57]
>
> —Trans high school student Kevin

each year and well over 50 percent of them feel physically unsafe at school.

The severity of anti-LGBTQ school violence varies from place to place and incident to incident. "I've been shoved into lockers, and sometimes people will just push up on me to check if I have boobs,"[57] says female-to-male trans high school student Kevin in Utah. When he complained to school administrators, he recalls, they told him it was his own fault for being open about his sexuality.

This type of response is more prevalent than many people realize. Larry, a gay college student in Massachusetts, grew up and attended high school in Kansas. He remembers witnessing three large football players shoving a young man half their size back and forth in a corridor between periods while a teacher watched. "The kid had been outed as gay the year before," he says.

> After that, his life at school was pretty miserable. Bigger guys were always sucker punching him when he was looking the other way, and he seemed to nearly always have a black eye. That time I saw the football jocks jump him, they threw him against the wall so hard he fell on the floor. They kicked him while he was down, and one of the social studies teachers saw it all and didn't do a damn thing to help him. He actually laughed right along with the jocks, and they all just left him there laying on the floor, holding his stomach, where they'd kicked him. I felt so bad for him, but I was also super-glad it wasn't me. Luckily, I was still in the closet then.[58]

Random Attacks

Violence against LGBTQ people is a problem not just in schools but also in almost all venues, including private homes, businesses, prisons, and diverse parts of the public sphere. Some cases involve random incidents in which someone attacks a stranger in a public place, such as on a street corner or in a store, bar, or movie theater. One of many recent examples took place in Jackson, Mississippi, in April 2019. The victim was twenty-eight-year-old Trevor Gray, a handsome, well-educated, and friendly individual who had stopped by a local bar to have a beer. While there, a burly man who had already had a few drinks invited the others at the bar, including Gray, to a get-together at a friend's house.

For reasons that are unclear, after everyone got to the house, the burly man became convinced that Gray was gay. After whispering something to a buddy, the burly man walked up to Gray and said, "What's up, bro?"[59] Not suspecting anything was amiss, Gray smiled and nodded his head. Suddenly, the burly man delivered a powerful sucker punch, striking Gray in the face

Brenda Scurlock holds a newspaper clipping about her daughter's murder. Her daughter, Chanel, was transgender. In June 2019, Chanel had gone out to see someone she had met on Facebook and was later found shot to death in a field.

Policies to Reduce Violent Bullying

According to Human Rights Watch, a major international humanitarian organization headquartered in New York City, comprehensive measures are needed to reduce the incidence of violent bullying in school, particularly against LGBTQ students. The organization recommends the following policies, which it believes will allow LGBTQ students to learn and socialize with straight teens without fear of violence:

> States should repeal outdated and stigmatizing laws that deter and arguably prohibit discussion of LGBTQ issues in schools, and enact laws protecting students and staff from bullying and discrimination based on sexual orientation and gender identity. Schools should ensure that policies, curricula, and resources explicitly include LGBTQ people, and that the school environment is responsive to the specific needs of LGBTQ youth. Teachers and administrators should work to make existing policies meaningful by enforcing protections and intervening when bullying or discrimination occurs.

Human Rights Watch, "Like Walking Through a Hailstorm," December 7, 2016. www.hrw.org.

and knocking him to the floor. The buddy then videotaped the burly man savagely beating Gray, punching his face at least seventeen times. Next, the buddy stopped the camera and he, too, pounded the now almost unconscious victim. No one present came to Gray's aid. After the attackers left him bleeding on the floor, he managed to drag himself to his car and drive to a nearby hospital. In addition to sustaining many cuts and bruises, his jaw was broken in two places and had to be wired shut for weeks.

Incredibly, Gray did not hold a grudge. "For as long as I can remember," he later told a newspaper reporter, "my family has taught me to see the best in others. My peace in this situation comes from that. So, for those wondering, I'm not angry or vengeful; I'm not sad. I'm optimistic. The events of that night are small when weighed against the incredible amount of love and support people have shown me."[60]

> **"I am proud to be me. I am proud to be trans."[61]**
>
> —An Instagram message posted by Missouri trans woman Ally Lee Steinfeld shortly before her murder

Preplanned Assaults

In many other cases, LGBTQ individuals are purposely targeted in advance and then are assaulted simply because they are not straight. A typical example was that of seventeen-year-old Ally Lee Steinfeld of Houston, Missouri, a male-to-female trans person. When her remains were found in a Missouri field, she officially became the twenty-first trans murder victim of 2017.

Despite being bullied often in school and called names by strangers on the street, in June of that year Steinfeld had posted on Instagram, "I am proud to be me. I am proud to be trans. I am beautiful. I don't care what people think."[61] What she did not

A mugshot shows the man charged with the 2017 murder of transgender teen Ally Lee Steinfeld. The man, along with two others, kidnapped Steinfeld and stabbed her to death.

know was that at the moment she posted that message, three young male residents of her town were already plotting to kill her. Convinced that trans people were freaks who did not deserve to live, the men kidnapped Steinfeld and brought her to the trailer one of them called home. First they tried to poison her. When that did not work, they stabbed her to death. Then they burned the

Getting to Some LGBTQ People

Eminent experts, including the members of the American Psychological Association, say that one of the key ways of reducing anti-LGBTQ hatred and violence is for decent, fair-minded straight people to educate other straight people to be more tolerant and humane. In a 2019 online article, the American Psychological Association explained that

> heterosexual people who wish to help reduce prejudice and discrimination can examine their own response to antigay stereotypes and prejudice. They can make a point of coming to know lesbian, gay and bisexual people, and they can work with lesbian, gay, and bisexual individuals and communities to combat prejudice and discrimination. Heterosexual individuals are often in a good position to ask other heterosexual people to consider the prejudicial or discriminatory nature of their beliefs and actions. Heterosexual allies can encourage nondiscrimination policies that include sexual orientation. They can work to make coming out safe. When lesbians, gay men and bisexual people feel free to make public their sexual orientation, heterosexuals are given an opportunity to have personal contact with openly gay people and to perceive them as individuals.
>
> Studies of prejudice, including prejudice against gay people, consistently show that prejudice declines when members of the majority group interact with members of a minority group. In keeping with this general pattern, one of the most powerful influences on heterosexuals' acceptance of gay people is having personal contact with an openly gay person. Antigay attitudes are far less common among members of the population who have a close [LGBTQ] friend or family member.

American Psychological Association, "Answers to Your Questions: For a Better Understanding of Sexual Orientation and Homosexuality," 2008. www.apa.org.

body and buried what was left of it near the trailer. The killers were later caught and punished.

Another preplanned assault on an LGBTQ person occurred in early December 2017 in Dallas, Texas. Three young men, who described themselves as straight, felt such hatred for gay people that they decided to kidnap and torture as many as they could. The men posted phony profiles (in which they pretended to be gay) on the dating app Grindr, a site that is frequented by LGBTQ individuals.

The perpetrators lured five gay men between the ages of nineteen and fifty-seven to an apartment complex and there held the victims at gunpoint for five days. During that time the kidnappers robbed the victims of their wallets, money, car keys, cars, driver's licenses, credit cards, and cell phones. The men also showered the victims with gay slurs, beat three of them, and sexually assaulted at least one of them. One of the kidnappers even urinated on a captive and smeared him with human feces. Finally, one of the victims managed to escape and notify authorities, who arrested the kidnappers.

Efforts to Reduce the Violence

Alarmed by the increasing incidence of such crimes against members of the LGBTQ community, a number of concerned individuals and groups have proposed ways of reducing the violence. Only a few of the national organizations engaged in this effort are the Family Equality Council, PFLAG (formerly Parents and Friends of Lesbians and Gays), the Trevor Project, and the Human Rights Campaign. All agree that one crucial remedy is improved education about LGBTQ people and their issues. The chief motivation for anti-LGBTQ violence is hate, they point out, and that hate is based mainly on ignorance regarding LGBTQ people.

There is also general agreement that unbiased information about human sexuality, including LGBTQ issues, should be routinely taught in school health classes. The aim of this information is to present the facts and thereby break down ugly, inaccurate stereotypes. As the leading authority on the subject of sexuality, the American Psychological Association, states,

> Both heterosexual behavior and homosexual behavior are normal aspects of human sexuality. Both have been documented in many different cultures and historical eras. Despite the persistence of stereotypes that portray lesbian, gay and bisexual people as disturbed, several decades of research and clinical experience have led all mainstream medical and mental health organizations in this country to conclude that these orientations represent normal forms of human experience. Lesbian, gay and bisexual relationships are normal forms of human bonding.[62]

Another vital approach to reducing and eventually eliminating anti-LGBTQ violence is to ensure that all such incidents—including those that result in deaths—are reported. Full, accurate, transparent reporting of the violence in the short run will help to reduce violence and save lives in the long run. This is the view of Congressman Sean Patrick Maloney, the first openly gay person elected to Congress from New York. Maloney says, "Victims of violence targeted at the LGBTQ community are often invisible to the rest of the world just because of who they are or who they love. We need quality data showing where, how, why, and to whom this violence is happening to [take] action and save LGBTQ lives."[63]

> **"Both heterosexual behavior and homosexual behavior are normal aspects of human sexuality."[62]**
>
> —American Psychological Association

To that end, Maloney introduced the LGBTQ Essential Data Act in June 2019. Once passed, that law will spend $25 million to revitalize outdated and underfunded data collection programs run by the Centers for Disease Control and Prevention. These programs collect and collate information from diverse local sources, including police reports, death certificates, coroner/medical examiner reports, and crime labs across the country. According to Human Right Campaign official David Stacy, "The *LGBTQ Essential Data Act* will give lawmakers and law enforcement the nec-

Sean Patrick Maloney (pictured), the first openly gay person elected to Congress from New York, introduced legislation designed to ensure that all anti-LGBTQ violence is properly reported.

essary tools to work toward justice and develop comprehensive legislative solutions to fight this epidemic."[64]

Efforts like Maloney's and those of the Human Rights Campaign and other humanitarian groups are part of the battle against anti-LGBTQ violence in the United States. Meanwhile, similar efforts are at work around the world because ignorance of and hatred for LGBTQ people (sometimes referred to as LGBTI, where *I* stands for *intersex*) exists virtually everywhere. Such efforts are essential, says a spokesperson for the human rights organization Amnesty International. "Bringing an end to homophobia and transphobia will save lives," he asserts. Moreover, "anti-LGBTI harassment puts LGBTI identifying people at a heightened risk of physical and psychological harm." The hatred and violence must end, he adds, because "everyone should be able to feel proud of who they are and who they love, [and] everyone has the right to life, freedom, and safety."[65]

> **"Everyone has the right to life, freedom, and safety."[65]**
>
> —Amnesty International

Source Notes

Introduction: Yearning for Equality

1. Larry, interview with the author, November 20, 2019.
2. Lesbian, Gay, Bisexual & Transgender Community Center, "What Is LGBTQ?" https://gaycenter.org.
3. Adi Barreto, "5 Things Your LGBTQ Co-Workers Wish You Knew," The Muse, 2019. www.themuse.com.
4. Pew Research Center, "Vast Majority of Americans Know Someone Who Is Gay, Fewer Know Someone Who Is Transgender," in *Where the Public Stands on Religious Liberty vs. Nondiscrimination,* September 28, 2016. www.pewforum.org.
5. Grace Hauck, "Anti-LGBT Hate Crimes Are Rising, the FBI Says," *USA Today,* July 1, 2019. www.usatoday.com.
6. Rebecca Damanti, "Can Education Reduce Prejudice Against LGBT People?," Century Foundation, 2016. https://tcf.org.
7. Human Rights Campaign, "Influencers and Celebrities Come Out for Equality in 2019," *HRC Blog,* 2019. www.hrc.org.

Chapter 1: Coming Out

8. Quoted in UCI Lesbian, Gay, Bisexual, Transgender Resource Center, "Coming Out Story No. 3," University of California, Irvine, Student Affairs. https://lgbtrc.uci.edu.
9. Trevor Support Center, "Bisexual," Trevor Project. www.thetrevorproject.org.
10. Trevor Support Center, "Bisexual."
11. Lesbian, Gay, Bisexual, Transgender, Queer Plus Resource Center, "Coming Out," University of Wisconsin–Milwaukee. www.uwm.edu.
12. Quoted in Pew Research Center, "The Coming Out Experience," in *A Survey of LGBT Americans: Attitudes, Experiences and Values in Changing Times,* June 13, 2013. www.pewsocialtrends.org.
13. Quoted in Pew Research Center, "The Coming Out Experience."

14. Quoted in UCI Lesbian, Gay, Bisexual, Transgender Resource Center, "Coming Out Story No. 1," University of California, Irvine, Student Affairs. https://lgbtrc.uci.edu.
15. Emily Bashforth, "11 Tips and Reminders for People Who Will Want to Come Out," Pride, October 11, 2019. www.pride.com.
16. Quoted in *The Lighthouse* (blog), "It's Science: Why Coming Out of the Closet Is Good for Your Health." http://blog.lighthouse.lgbt.
17. Quoted in *The Lighthouse* (blog), "It's Science."
18. Morgana Bailey, "TED Talk: On Coming Out," TED, November 2014. www.ted.com.
19. Quoted in Pew Research Center, "The Coming Out Experience."
20. Quoted in Pew Research Center, "The Coming Out Experience."
21. Quoted in Pew Research Center, "The Coming Out Experience."
22. Quoted in Human Rights Campaign, "Influencers and Celebrities Come Out for Equality in 2019."

Chapter 2: Challenges for Young People

23. ULifeline, "Emotional Challenges Faced by LGBTQ Students." www.ulifeline.org.
24. Sejal Singh and Laura E. Durso, "Widespread Discrimination Continues to Shape LGBT People's Lives in Both Subtle and Significant Ways," Center for American Progress, May 2, 2017. www.americanprogress.org.
25. Quoted in Christine Jackson-Taylor, "For LGBT People, Life Can Be Full of Small Daily Struggles," World Economic Forum, July 11, 2018. www.weforum.org.
26. Shabab Ahmed Mirza and Frank J. Bewkes, "Secretary DeVos Is Failing to Protect the Civil Rights of LGBTQ Students," Center for American Progress, July 29, 2019. www.americanprogress.org.
27. Quoted in Clare Kenny, "LGBTQ Youth Share Their Stories, Offer Advice to Adults to End Bullying," GLAAD, October 18, 2018. www.glaad.org.

28. Quoted in Kenny, "LGBTQ Youth Share Their Stories, Offer Advice to Adults to End Bullying."
29. Quoted in Kara Lowe, "Queer Students Navigate Dating Scene," Student Printz, November 15, 2019. www.studentprintz.com.
30. Quoted in Ellen Friedrichs, "Dating Tips for Gay Teens," Live About, April 13, 2018. www.liveabout.com.
31. Friedrichs, "Tips for Gay Teens Who Want a Boyfriend."
32. Friedrichs, "Tips for Gay Teens Who Want a Boyfriend."
33. Quoted in Friedrichs, "Tips for Gay Teens Who Want a Boyfriend."
34. Friedrichs, "Tips for Gay Teens Who Want a Boyfriend."
35. Friedrichs, "Tips for Gay Teens Who Want a Boyfriend."
36. ULifeline, "Emotional Challenges Faced by LGBTQ Students."
37. ULifeline, "Emotional Challenges Faced by LGBTQ Students."
38. Quoted in ULifeline, "Emotional Challenges Faced by LGBTQ Students."
39. Quoted in ULifeline, "Emotional Challenges Faced by LGBTQ Students."

Chapter 3: Creating a Family

40. Quoted in Abigail Woodruff and Jutta Tobias, "Lesbian and Gay Parents," Society for the Psychological Study of Social Issues, December 2009. www.spssi.org/_data/n_0001/resources/live/SPSSI%20Factsheet_LG%20Parents%20v2.pdf.
41. Woodruff and Tobias, "Lesbian and Gay Parents."
42. Quoted in Corinne Lightweaver, "Children of LGBT Parents Speak Out for the Let Love Define Family Series," *Huffington Post,* December 6, 2017. www.huffpost.com.
43. Quoted in Lightweaver, "Children of LGBT Parents Speak Out for the Let Love Define Family Series."
44. George, interview with the author, November 27, 2019.
45. Quoted in What We Know: The Public Policy Research Portal, "What Does the Scholarly Research Say About the Well-Being

of Children with Gay or Lesbian Parents?," Cornell University. https://whatweknow.inequality.cornell.edu.
46. GayAdoption.org, "Gay Adoption Facts." https://gayadoption.org.
47. Quoted in Lightweaver, "Children of LGBT Parents Speak Out for the Let Love Define Family Series."

Chapter 4: At Work and in the Public Sphere

48. Quoted in Singh and Durso, "Widespread Discrimination Continues to Shape LGBT People's Lives in Both Subtle and Significant Ways."
49. Quoted in Singh and Durso, "Widespread Discrimination Continues to Shape LGBT People's Lives in Both Subtle and Significant Ways."
50. Quoted in Singh and Durso, "Widespread Discrimination Continues to Shape LGBT People's Lives in Both Subtle and Significant Ways."
51. Catalyst, *Quick Take: Lesbian, Gay, Bisexual, and Transgender Workplace Issues*, June 17, 2019. www.catalyst.org.
52. Jay Michaelson, "Transgender Panic Isn't Hate—It's Ignorance," Daily Beast, April 13, 2017. www.thedailybeast.com.
53. Arthur, interview with the author, December 2, 2019.
54. Dylan, interview with the author, December 5, 2019.
55. Quoted in Frankie Wallace, "Going to the Doctor as a Transgender Patient," *The Humanist,* September 11, 2018. https://thehumanist.com.

Chapter 5: Faced with Violence

56. Quoted in CBS News, "FBI: Hate Crime Murders Hit Record in 2018; Crimes Targeting Transgender People Soar," November 12, 2019. www.cbsnews.com.
57. Quoted in Human Rights Watch, "Like Walking Through a Hailstorm," December 7, 2016. www.hrw.org.
58. Larry, interview.
59. Quoted in Sarah Fowler, "'It Wouldn't Matter If He Was': Man Beaten Because They Thought He was Gay, Family Says," *Clarion Ledger,* April 18, 2019. www.clarionledger.com.

60. Quoted in Fowler, "'It Wouldn't Matter If He Was.'"
61. Quoted in Anna Swartz, "Ally Lee Steinfeld Is at Least the 21st Transgender Person Killed So Far in 2017," Mic, September 26, 2017. www.mic.com.
62. American Psychological Association, "Answers to Your Questions: For a Better Understanding of Sexual Orientation and Homosexuality," 2008. www.apa.org.
63. Quoted in Trevor Project, "Maloney Introduces LGBTQ Essential Data Act to Combat Deadly Violence Against LGBTQ Community," *Trevor News* (blog), June 13, 2019. www.thetrevorproject.org.
64. Quoted in Trevor Project, "Maloney Introduces LGBTQ Essential Data Act to Combat Deadly Violence Against LGBTQ Community."
65. Amnesty International, "LGBTI Rights." www.amnesty.org.

Organizations and Websites

Family Equality Council—www.familyequality.org

The Family Equality Council supports and represents the 3 million parents who are gay, bi, trans, and queer in the United States and their 6 million children. The website offers information on how ordinary people, both straight and LGBTQ, can combat anti-LGBTQ discrimination in their communities.

Genders & Sexualities Alliance (GSA) Network
https://gsanetwork.org

The GSA Network's strategy is to fight for justice for LGBTQ people by empowering teens and others to educate the public on LGBTQ issues. The site offers a hands-on tutorial of how young LGBTQ people can build their own local support networks.

Gender Spectrum—www.genderspectrum.org

The Gender Spectrum works with families, private groups, and public institutions with the aim of making society more welcoming for transgender people. The website features how-to guides that trans individuals can use as tools to create more gender inclusive spaces in their workplaces and communities.

Human Rights Campaign (HRC)—www.hrc.org

The HRC deals regularly and frankly with gay, bi, and trans issues and problems. The site offers an array of links to articles that tell what is happening on the front lines of the LGBTQ struggle for equality, broken down on a convenient, easy-to-access, and state-by-state basis.

National Center for Transgender Equality
http://transequality.org

The organization's mission is to help trans people enjoy equality and social justice, partly by educating politicians and other leaders about trans issues. The website contains helpful information about how trans and other LGBTQ people can lobby their representatives in Congress as well as obtain health insurance.

PFLAG—www.pflag.org

Formerly known as Parents and Friends of Lesbians and Gays, PFLAG has worked tirelessly since its founding in 1972 to promote equality for and decent treatment of LGBTQ people. Its website features links to articles about current events affecting gay, bi, and trans people, along with information on how to work directly with one of the group's four hundred national chapters.

Transgender Legal Defense and Education Fund
www.transgenderlegal.org

The Transgender Legal Defense and Education Fund opposes bias and discrimination based on gender/sexual identity and thereby promotes equality for all Americans, whether LGBTQ or straight. The website contains information on how people can obtain internships in the group's public work.

Trevor Project—www.trevorproject.org

The Trevor Project is the leading national organization providing crisis intervention and suicide prevention services to LGBTQ people under the age of twenty-five. The website contains contact information for individuals and groups that can help LGBTQ youth in crisis.

For Further Research

Books

Kathleen Archambeau, *Pride and Joy: LGBTQ Artists, Icons, and Everyday Heroes.* Miami: Mango, 2017.

Leanne Currie-McGhee, *LGBT Families*. San Diego: ReferencePoint, 2019.

Lelaina Erikson, *Unconditional: A Guide to Loving and Supporting Your LGBTQ Child.* Miami: Mango, 2017.

Heidi C. Feldman, *LGBT Discrimination*. San Diego: ReferencePoint, 2019.

Lee-Anne Gray, *LGBTQ Youth: A Guided Workbook to Support Sexual Orientation and Gender Identity.* Eau-Claire, WI: PESI, 2018.

Eric Rosswood and Kathleen Archambeau, *We Make It Better: The LGBTQ Community and Their Positive Contributions to Society.* Miami: Mango, 2019.

Robyn Ryle, *Throw Like a Girl, Cheer Like a Boy: The Evolution of Gender, Identity, and Race in Sports.* Lanham, MD: Rowman and Littlefield, 2020.

Susan Stryker, *Transgender History.* New York: Seal, 2017.

Internet Sources

American Adoptions, "LGBTQ Adoption: Can Same-Sex Couples Adopt?" www.americanadoptions.com.

Tina Fetner, "U.S. Attitudes Toward Lesbian and Gay People Are Better than Ever," *Contexts,* June 22, 2016. https://journals.sagepub.com.

GLSEN, "Coming Out: A Resource for LGBTQ Students," 2019. www.glsen.org.

Katie Langin, "'Now I Know I'm Not Alone.' Study Highlights Challenges LGBTQ Workers in STEM Face," *Science*, June 13, 2019. www.sciencemag.org.

Lesbian, Gay, Bisexual & Transgender Community Center, "What Is LGBTQ?" https://gaycenter.org.

Sarah McBride, "HRC Releases Annual Report on Epidemic of Anti-Transgender Violence." *HRC Blog,* Human Rights Campaign, November 18, 2019. www.hrc.org.

Diego Sanchez, "Hate Crime Statistics and Prevention," PFLAG. https://pflag.org.

Prince Shakur, "LGBTQ Icons You Need to Know: And How to Find More," *Teen Vogue,* June 27, 2017.

David Spiegelhalter, "Is 10% of the Population Really Gay?," *The Guardian* (Manchester, UK), March 21, 2018. www.theguardian.com.

Trevor Support Center, "Bisexual," Trevor Project. www.thetrevorproject.org.

Daniel Trotta, "Some 4.5 Percent of U.S. Adults Identify as LGBT: Study," Reuters, March 5, 2019. www.reuters.com.

UCI Lesbian, Gay, Bisexual, Transgender Resource Center, "Coming Out Stories." University of California, Irvine, Student Affairs. https://lgbtrc.uci.edu.

Zachary Zane, "7 Ways to Support a Friend Who's Questioning Their Sexuality," Pride, July 14, 2019. www.pride.com.

Index

Picture Credits

Cover: loreanto/Shutterstock

6: oneinchpunch/Shutterstock
10: Sandra van der Steen/Shutterstock
13: Marian Fil/Shutterstock
16: lev radin/Shutterstock
21: LightField Studios/Shutterstock
23: WAYHOME studio/Shutterstock
27: Monkey business images/Shutterstock
33: Africa Studio/Shutterstock
38: Rob Crandall/Shutterstock.com
40: DGLimages/Shutterstocl.com
45: fitzcrittle/Shutterstock
49: lofti photography/Shutterstock
52: Monkey Business Images/Shutterstock
57: Associated Press
59: Associated Press
63: Associated Press

About the Author

In addition to his numerous acclaimed volumes on ancient civilizations, historian Don Nardo has published several studies of medical and scientific discoveries and phenomena. Among these are *Cardiovascular Disease, Germs, Eating Disorders, Polar Explorations, Black Holes, Ice Ages, Climate Change, Science and Sustainable Energy,* and *Nanotechnology and Medicine.* Mr. Nardo also composes and arranges orchestral music. He lives with his wife, Christine, in Massachusetts.